THE KEYS TO DIRECT SALES SUCCESS

MICHAEL J MANLEY

authorHOUSE®

AuthorHouse™
1663 Liberty Drive
Bloomington, IN 47403
www.authorhouse.com
Phone: 1-800-839-8640

First published by AuthorHouse 10/14/2009

ISBN: 978-1-4490-1960-0 (sc)
ISBN: 978-1-4490-1961-7 (hc)

Library of Congress Control Number: 2009908756

Printed in the United States of America
Bloomington, Indiana

This book is printed on acid-free paper.

To the memory of Laurel Douglas (Doug) Greer (1952–2001), the most incredible salesperson I have ever known, a true master of this trade, and a best friend.

To Harry Hedges, the only one in my life who really took time sales training with me. He is a true sales professional and a best friend. Whatever sales success I may have, I owe to him.

2008/1/5 5:42

To Drew Ramsey, who inspired this book. Drew is eighty years old. He was new to the direct sales specialty that I do, and he got right in my face and demanded I show him how to do this and to write it down. I couldn't say no. This book is the result.

CONTENTS

PREFACE

Throughout this book, you will see many photos of my direct sales, actual customers that I have sold to in their homes. It was important for me to put them in this book to demonstrate my credibility that I actually do this for real. Many sales books are just philosophical or concepts, but they never did it. This one lives. When you look at these pictures, notice a few things:

- My customers are happy. They had a good experience.
- In many of the photos, I am wearing the same shirt. I made many of the sales on the same day.
- In many photos, you can see me sitting around the kitchen table with my presentation book open, showing a direct sale.

Most importantly, all of these photos were taken over a one-month period. That's right. I made one hundred individual sales in a month. If you sell one hundred of anything in one month, you'll be just fine. This book tells you how it's done.

INTRODUCTION

Selling at the top of the leaderboard is easy if you follow the simple steps in this book. As a salesperson or someone thinking about a career in sales, you will only want to be at one place, the point of sale. You may be asking yourself:

- What is it?
- Where is it?
- How do I get there?
- How do I find it?
- How will I know for sure when I'm there?
- And what do you do when it arrives?

The point of sale is the very moment when you have made your money. It's kind of like hitting three aces on a slot machine by skill, not by luck, so you better be ready. There is absolutely no doubt that, by following and studying the process of the master keys, you will be ready and guaranteed to be at the point of sale successfully every time.

Over the past thirty years, I have been to just about every sales training school, seminar, boot camp, academy, or institute. I sometimes came away with at least one good thing, but they were mostly a waste of time, especially when the instructor never really actually did the job or sold a thing in his or her life. But, then again, they were fun times.

I am a door-to-door, around-the-kitchen-table salesman, but I am special because I am the best there is in the world. Well, at least I think so, because if I don't, no one else will! In 1987, I was the top salesman in the United States in my product line for a major insurance company. This is out of about fifty thousand agents or so. Since then, I have won every award that the companies I have represented offer, including trophies, plaques, cash, prizes, and trips all over the world.

I am glad I won so many plaques. Not so long ago, an ice storm hit the Northeast, where I was living at the time, and the power went out. After a while, it began to be a very serious matter. It began to start freezing in the house. We had a fireplace, but just a few logs, so I used many of the plaques to keep the fire going. It worked until the power was turned on. The moral of this little story is that it's good to win plaques.

Over the years, even to this day, I have stayed at the top with different companies and different products. In this book, I stay away from what I think or my opinion about a successful direct sales process. I stay focused on what you must do with no argument or debate. The master keys covered in this book include knowledge, confidence, practice, presentation, perpetual close, discipline, following success, and having fun. When you finish this book, you will have all the tools to be number one and stay at the top as well. No one will ever be able to take it from you.

Because of my successes, I was always selected for management, first on a district level, then a regional level, then a state level, and then to a multiple-state territory. What I am about to tell may be one of the most important self-examination and awareness decisions you will ever make about yourself in your sales career. When we work through all the master keys in this book and apply them in real life, you will find out what you are really good at. Sometimes, it may not be what you thought, as in my case. When you start in a career, begin to achieve some successes, and then be offered a so-called promotion to management, it feels great. It pumps up the ego, and you are eager to take on the challenge. Truthfully, I wasn't a very good manager at all, and I never really liked it. I really couldn't believe all the BS there is and all the jerks there are. I never really held anything against any of the jerks I had to deal with because they had to deal with even bigger jerks and on and on. Only later in my career did I really figure that out.

◆ Game Theory vs. Direct Sale

Game theory is a science that studies and applies mathematical models and assumptions that offers a tractable way of predicting outcomes. To come up with this definition, I summed up some very lengthy and complicated ones, but that is basically it. According to my definition, direct sales theory is a science that involves many human interactions, emotion and communication skills, and everything in this book. That's basically it.

In short, the difference between a sales manager and a direct salesperson at any level is game theory. Basically, the sales manager is all about game theory, that is, the numbers and only the numbers. This, in most cases, at least as far as I'm concerned, is a very cold and sometimes ruthless existence. I called these management positions "T-ball jobs" because your head is like a ball on a tee that it will eventually get whacked off of. I really don't know anyone who kept a management position for very long. Because of this, the turnover is incredible, except if you are related to the owners. I would often wonder how anything could get done. I have often said that I wished I had all the business these companies lost because of these jerks. I would be featured on the *Forbes* list of the richest men in the world.

Along the way, the day will come when you will discover what you are not. It will make you humble, and you will have to face that reality head-on, but on that day, it will be one of the best days of your life. When you find out who you are, find your place in this sales world, and hone your skills, you will leave everyone in the dust and reap the rewards. Today, to be promoted in sales management, I think that is punishment for a job well done. I just can't be that cold or ruthless to anyone, and I don't want to be. I'm much better off doing what I do best. I may not be the best manager in the world or even close, nor do I care to be. But when it comes to the profession of direct sales, I wrote the book.

With all the sales training and experience I have had over the years, only a few fundamentals and techniques are master keys to your sales success and absolutely work every single time. You must absolutely follow this order. It will bring you to the point of sale every time. So let's take the time and dig deep into this together. When we finish, you will be guaranteed to succeed.

CHAPTER ONE

THE REALITY

Because you have chosen sales as a profession or are thinking about sales as a profession, you should at least know what you are talking about when you are presenting your product? Don't you agree? Apparently, there are a lot of people who don't!

To this day, several industries are suffering miserably with this problem, and you don't need to be an industry analyst to point it out when you can experience it firsthand yourself. Probably many more industries have this problem other than the few I mention here, but let's take a look at what I'm talking about and see if you agree.

♦ Auto Industry

Have you ever walked into an auto dealership, met up with a salesperson, spent some time talking about the car you are interested in buying, and only then quickly determine that the salesperson doesn't really know much about the cars at all? It happens to me almost every time. So I take the manufacturer's brochure and read it. It pretty much tells me everything I need to know. I then leave the dealership with the brochures, review my options at home, and never return to see that salesperson again. That person lost my sale, and that company lost my business possibly for life.

♦ Computer Industry

A car is much easer to operate than a computer. If you just go to any computer store, you will see for yourself. You walk into a PC store or outlet, meet up with a salesperson, spend some time talking about what you are interested in, and then only quickly determine that the salesperson has gone so far past your comprehension level in a second that there really is no use in talking anymore. So you go to look at the TVs because you don't want to appear as stupid as you are. That idiot lost my sale, and that company lost my business, possibly for life.

♦ Tire Industry

Did you ever go into to a tire store, talk to the salesperson, and try to figure what tire would be the best for your car? There are about a gazillion of them. In this case, you don't even try much. You just say yes, try to get the best price, look dumb, and pay because you need that tire. You don't have much of a choice. I call that sales process the wham-bam-thank-you-ma'am process. It's not much of a process at all. In some cases with some products, that's just the way it is. It's also the reason to purchase over the Internet. That person got my sale, but that company lost my business, possibly for life.

♦ Heating and Air-conditioning Industry

Last year, my air-conditioner went on the blink. I had a service contract, and the HVAC company came around every year to service my unit. So I called them to fix my AC. The guy came to the house, walked to the closet with the air handler in it, opened the door, and immediately said, "You need a new air handler."

I said, "Do you have any job openings for guys who do what you do?"

He asked, "What do you mean?"

I said, "Well, I can go around on these calls and tell people they just need a new one all day long without even looking at it."

I then impolitely asked him to leave. Needless to say, that idiot lost my sale, and that company lost my business for life

♦ Insurance Industry

So you sit down to look into an insurance policy. The salesperson doesn't seem to know enough to win your confidence, or he or she seems to know so much that you are so lost you become uncomfortable and start thinking, "There must be something wrong here. I'm going to get ripped off." So what do you do? You go to the kitchen, pull out the magnifying glass, and try to read the small print. Even then, you can't read it. Then you turn the policy over to make sure nothing is written that way, just to make sure. That person lost my sale, and that company lost my business for life.[1]

All of these sales experiences of mine are just the beginning of the stories that are out there, including your own. These examples only resulted in one thing, a dissatisfied customer. Importantly, every one of these stories and countless others like them could have been prevented. Here is where the master keys come into play. As we go through all the master keys together, we can later revisit these sales examples and see how a dissatisfied customer would have been a satisfied customer. Remember these master keys must be a part of every sales presentation. Let's look at knowledge.

---

[1]   During World War I, a life insurance company sold life insurance policies to soldiers just before going off to war. When a surviving family member of a deceased soldier made a claim for the life insurance, the company denied the claim. The company said the policy was void in time of war, and this was clearly stated on the back of the policy, upside down in Spanish. Because of an uproar from the surviving families, the insurance department was born.

CHAPTER TWO

THE FIRST MASTER KEY: KNOWLEDGE

Webster's defines "knowledge" as:

- "Knowledge or abilities gained through being educated"
- "The imparting and acquiring of knowledge through teaching and learning, especially at a school or similar institution"

You would think that knowing your product would be understood, but it just isn't the case in today's world. You become a salesperson because of what you know, not because of your God-given personality. In fact, the more you know about something, the more personality you have. And that holds true for everyone!

◆ The Knitting Lady

Not so long ago, I sold a policy to a wonderful, young lady of eighty-four years in her home while she was quietly knitting. While we were wrapping things up, she paused and said, "You know, young man, you are one of the best salesman I ever met. I was never good at sales."

Naturally, I loved hearing that. Noticing she was knitting, I replied, "You know, young lady, you're the best knitter I ever met. I was never good at that."

Naturally, she loved hearing that. So I started asking her a few questions about knitting. She suddenly lit up like stadium lights on a baseball field. She began telling me everything you could possibly want to know about knitting, from its very origin to today's latest technology. Needless to say, she had me sold. She had me so captivated that I had to cancel the rest of my appointments that day because I was there so long.

When I finally left, I turned to her and said, "Ya know, not only are you the best knitting person I've ever known, you're the best saleslady I ever met."

She just loved hearing that, but it was true. The appointment ended with a hug.

This story is power-packed for sales analysis. All the master keys were in play. Undoubtedly, the knowledge key worked for me, but the knowledge key worked for her as well. Interestingly, this lady had this knowledge about her craft that no one could take from her, and it showed. She was one of the best in sales and didn't even know it. As she sat there quietly knitting, her God-given personality really became vibrant when she was asked about something she really knew about. Everything in sales stems from knowledge.

♦ Take Time to Learn Your Product

I can guarantee you that every time I speak to a group about this master key knowledge and I ask a random person about something stated in his or her company's product brochures, he or she won't know it.

You must take the time to learn everything you can about the product you are presenting to sell. Some products take longer to study than others will. You need to know the origin and history of that product. Most companies or manufacturers supply brochures, owner's manuals, and even videos. You must take the time to look at them. Someone once said to me, "The only thing new is the history you don't know." I have found that to be so true in so many situations. You need to take it apart and put it back together again. Yes, where possible, you should physically take it apart and put it back together again. You should go to the manufacturer, tour the assembly, attend the manufacturer's classes, or at least watch their video. You need to be tested on it. You need to test yourself on it. You need to know it better than anyone else because you will surely lose a sale if you don't. Your kinks in your armor will kill you when they are exposed.

Now let's step it up a notch. You should know your competitors' product just as well as you know your own.

◆ Abbreviations

I always got a kick out of all the abbreviations on business cards: DSC, RSC, SSC, LU, LUTCF, PhD, and so forth. I guess it's important that you know that they have some knowledge even before they start talking, even though most people don't know what most of them mean.

I thought I should have something on my card as well. I wanted it to be reflective of what I really was. So I added on "PPC" and "HC" to the end of my name. I think it looks pretty impressive. "PPC" means "professional porch climber," and "HC" means "humor consultant" because that was what I actually did and that was who I actually was. It was the best inside joke of the day among those who knew me. I think the funniest part of the whole thing was that nobody ever asked me what it meant. Just think of all the money I saved by not going to get all those other abbreviations. It's not about the impressive degrees you have on your card. It's how well you know your product.

◆ When You Don't Know Something

I know my product pretty darn well, but somebody occasionally asks a question that I don't know the answer to. I know that's hard to believe, but it's true. In this situation, you need to say, "I don't have the answer to that, but I'll find out and get right back to you." If you try to bluff it, people can instinctively see right through you, and you will lose.

◆ When You Really Know Something

My six-year military experience in the United States Army Infantry is a great example about knowledge saving your life. The military does a great job of making sure you know what you are doing because your life will depend on it, and there is an order to things. In the infantry, your constant companion is your M16 automatic rifle. You actually sleep with it. The army will teach you everything there is to know about that weapon. Not only will you know how to fire it, but you will also know how to take it apart and put it back together again. You must also pass their test to do it blindfolded. That's a pretty good example of knowing a product. It's a great analogy to sales because you must know everything about your product. It is your livelihood, and your life depends on it. You need to take the time to know your product inside and out, no matter how long it takes.

♦ A Review

Don't even try until you know what you're talking about. Everyone is comfortable when he or she feels he or she has made a well-informed decision. This is your job. This all goes back to the basic definition of knowledge. Knowledge is acquired through teaching and learning, and it gives you the ability to be educated. Take the time to know everything you can about your product. Then you will see how that knowledge leads to confidence.

THE SECOND MASTER KEY: CONFIDENCE

There is something almost magical about the second-most absolute fundamental, confidence. Not only do you need to have it on the inside, but it also shows on the outside. People seem to think this is the hardest one of all because it has to do with overcoming so many things like fear, nerves, self-consciousness, pressure, stage fright, worry, and so forth. But this is the easiest one of the master keys of all, and it happens by itself.

Webster's says that "confidence" is:

- "Self-assurance or a belief in your ability to succeed"
- "The belief or trust in somebody or something or in the ability of somebody or something to act in a proper, trustworthy, or reliable manner."

Three keywords are jumping out at me: self-assurance, ability, and reliable. I like those three words, and so will your prospect. You will need them in your back pocket on your road to success.

♦ The Cornstalk Lady

I once took a very attractive, very well-dressed lady with me on a sales call at a home. All the managers would have the new people ride with me for a day or two to see a pro in action. After being acquainted, we started talking about the business at hand. She started telling me about how nervous she was. So I took some time and went over everything. I assured her that everything would be fine and not to worry. She really was nervous. Her hands were shaking, and she couldn't sit still.

We went to a farmhouse sitting at the end of a long driveway. The house was surrounded by cornfields that went on for as far as we could see. As we approached the door, she kept saying how nervous she was. I kept saying that she shouldn't worry about anything. I rang the doorbell. Right after, she ran away like a crazy person running for her life, way out into the cornfields. You should have seen the expression on my face when the prospect answered the door. I could not contain this giggling smirk on my face. I went in the house anyway and made the sale.

While I was making my presentation, she came out of the cornfields and hid in the backseat of my car. When I came out to my car, I heard a voice say, "Just drive away. Hurry! I'm okay." I drove down the road and pulled into a gas station so she could gain her composure.

As she got out of the backseat, I could see that she broke one of her heels, her hose was ripped, her dress had dirt stains all up one side, and some scratches were on her arms. As we both looked back into the backseat of my new Lincoln, we saw two cornstalks. At that moment, there was an outburst of laughter that is still going on today. I took her home so she could freshen up and change. Then I took her back to the office. Later that evening, her sales manager called to ask how she did that day. I said she was, by far, one of the best-trained recruits that came out of his office in quite a while and she was off to a great start. That was the joke of the day, knowing how much he had ahead of him with her.

Now this story is power-packed for sales analysis as well. All the master keys were in play here for knowledge and confidence. No matter how extreme this story seems to be, it really happened. Do you think we have an issue with confidence here? I think so.

Confidence is magical. It creates itself based on knowledge and continues to build by itself indefinitely. It's kind of like the natural evolution of things. Confidence, as it pertains to sales, evolves and expresses itself entirely based on the depth of knowledge you have about your product and the experience you gain along the way.

The eighty-four-year-old knitting lady was so confident about her craft because she knew just about everything about it. She had the knowledge. The knowledge made her confident. It's automatic. However, in the case of the cornstalk lady, I don't think she knew much about anything that day. In the simplest terms, if you know what you are talking about, you will be confident, and it will show.

♦ A Mentor

A mentor is a wise and faithful counselor. When I was starting out in direct sales, I had a mentor by the name of Harry Hedges. Simply put, he was just a great guy. It really is special when you have had a mentor in your life because you never forget that person and you always look back fondly. Usually, there is someone who helps you get started, but he or she doesn't always stick with you. You are really lucky if he or she does.

When you are starting with a new product, you should ask the person who is helping you if he or she would be your mentor. If so, great! If not, ask someone who would. It's a great way to get going and make a lifelong friend. Some companies actually assign you one, but that doesn't always work out. It's best when you find someone you are comfortable with. Harry taught me many things, especially the intricacies and nuances of professional selling. You will see how they play a significant part in selling as we go along.

♦ Oh, Harry!

Harry spent a lot of time getting me ready for selling. He must have seen something in me, but he knew I needed some work. One day, Harry took me out on one of my first sales call in a home. He was going to show me how it was done. I was only to observe and say nothing. The lady was in her mid-seventies, and she had emphysema. She had two giant oxygen tanks in her living room, and the oxygen tube attached around her head went all around the room and passed very visibly right under my feet.

Harry was very good. While he was making his presentation, he would look over at me very briefly from time to time to see if I were following. I would concur with a quick nod. Harry was soon at the point of sale, a very serious and controlled time. He began to exercise his first close, one of many you will also learn in this book. As he delivered his first close, he looked over at me to see if I caught it. As he was looking at me, I simultaneously began applying pressure on the lady's oxygen tube with my foot. I wasn't actually stepping on the tube or applying any pressure at all, but from across the room, it looked like I was.

When Harry saw that, you could see this big smile come across his face. Moments later, when Harry realized what I was doing jokingly, cutting off her oxygen to assist him in his close of the sale, he tried, but he could not contain himself. During his attempt at containment, he would inadvertently begin to snort like a pig. Then snot began to shoot from his nose. His face turned red, and he began to choke. He had a complete meltdown. He had to excuse himself, and he stepped outside to regain his composure, which he never could. All of this was right at the point of sale. It was so funny that the laughter continues to this day. Harry got the sale. That day, I got a boost in confidence and realized how much fun selling could be.

This principle applies in pretty much anything you decide to take on, even if it's your hobby. I recently took up flying remote control airplanes, as in remote control jets. This can be a very expensive hobby. These little jets have real, miniature turbine jet engines. Some cost from $10,000 to over $50,000. It is absolute amazing to see them fly. It's also amazing to see them crash and see a grown man cry. I don't think you would attempt to fly one of these if you didn't know what you were doing because you will crash.

Your sales presentation is the same thing. If you don't know what you're doing, you will crash. On the other hand, if you take the time to study and gain the knowledge all about the jet, you will begin to gain confidence. With several hours of practice on a little home flight simulator, you will be ready to fly. It's the same thing in sales. If you get the knowledge, you will know your product. You will begin to feel confident because the knowledge leads to confidence, but in this case, as in the case of any product, you are going to need to practice, practice, and practice.

◆ Loss of Confidence

Not so long ago, I was going on an appointment that I had confirmed. I really needed to make that sale. I really needed the money, and I was feeling great about the appointment. So I was driving along, and a fire truck and ambulance were blaring their sirens behind. Naturally, I pulled over. As I was going along my way, I noticed on my GPS that I was about ten minutes away. I turned into a very large neighborhood with lots of streets, curves, and turns. I couldn't help but notice that the fire truck and ambulance I was following were making the same turns as I was. Sure enough, when it came to the last street I was to turn on, the fire truck and ambulance turned there as well. The fire truck and ambulance went right to the house where I had an appointment. My prospect came out on the stretcher.

What are the chances of something like that happening? It is safe to say that I lost all confidence that day. When something like that happens, it's sometimes better to just go home and take a nap. This really happened. I even took a photo from my truck window (see below).

When I was writing this book one day, I was working for about ten hours straight. I am not a book-writing type of person. I'm not even close. As simple as you think this book may be, you need to know that it was a monumental task for me. I was really into it that day, and I really wrote a lot. It was the most I ever had written in one sitting, and I was really proud of myself. Later that night, I was tired. Before I went to bed, I went to turn off the computer. As I closed out Microsoft Word, the computer asked if I wanted to save the changes I had made. I pushed no. I lost everything I wrote, and it could not be retrieved. I even paid two different companies to try to retrieve it, and they could not. I was simply beside myself and in total disbelief. I had a total loss of confidence, but the book is here.

♦ A Review

To be self-assured is to know what you are talking about. Knowledge leads to confidence. This confidence creates a belief in yourself and the ability for you to succeed. It seems like there is always something that comes along that will shake your confidence in different ways. But knowledge is something you own, and it cannot be taken away from you. When you know your craft really well, you will always bounce back from any adversity. That's how confident you need to be, and it will show on your face.

CHAPTER FOUR

THE THIRD MASTER KEY: PRACTICE

◆ Practice, Practice, Practice

Before you can smoothly transition to your product presentation from your greeting time in the real world, you need to practice, practice, and practice. Webster's says that "practice" is:

- "Doing something repeatedly in order to improve performance"
- "The process of repeating something many times in order to improve performance"
- "The process of carrying out an idea, plan, or theory"
- "An established way of doing something, especially one that has developed through experience and knowledge"
- "In the real world under everyday conditions, as opposed to in theory"

Yielding to the definition, I really like the last definition of "in the real world under everyday conditions." Don't you just hate it when some jerk from the company is telling you how to do something and pounding on you in a training setting and he or she never did it himself or herself? It's no longer theory; it's for real now. The primary reason to practice and practice and practice before you go out in the real world is to minimize your mistakes. You will still make some mistakes in your presentations when you first go out, but when a big commission is on the line, you won't make the same mistake twice. This preparation can take days, weeks, or even months, depending on the product and you. The knowledge you now have and the time you took to prepare will exude confidence in the real world. Do not go out unless you are prepared to the best of your abilities. The better prepared you are before you go out, the sooner you can fine-tune your presentation to perfection. Then (and only then) will you be able to really hone in and be a master at the point of sale.

♦ At the Practice Stage

You need to gather up everything you can to make your product presentation: a presentation binder, handouts, a laptop with a PowerPoint presentation, or a projector, just to name a few. You should try to find convenient things to transport these things in. The company usually has prepared many things to help you as well. You should try to get your hands on everything you can and work with it all until you find the right combination of these tools that works best for you. When you think you have it down, you should try it on someone and see what he or she says. Then you should work out the kinks. You can even film yourself giving your presentation. You can be your own critic. You should always save the first film clip so you can look back in a few years to get a big laugh. You should keep doing this until you think you have it near perfect. You should always try to streamline. That is, you shouldn't drag something out too long. You should be mindful of time. When you start to do this, you will quickly find yourself instinctively putting things in an organized order for your presentation. Your goal is to communicate to your client in an easy, simple, step-by-step process and bring it to a close.

There is an old saying in this business, "Keep it simple, stupid." It's very true. The computer people are the absolute worst violators of this. They seem to thrive on making you feel stupid within the first ten seconds of meeting them, and they will continue to do so throughout their little presentations. They want to make sure they show you their computer wizardry stuff while they lose you to the TV section the whole time. I stopped one of them once and said, "Perhaps you should ask me how familiar I am with this product and then go from there."

This is a very good way to open your transition to your product presentation. This question can also be very instrumental in setting the pace of your presentation. You need to break your product down for presentation, somewhat like a product brochure. You should look at how the product is introduced and progressively laid out. You begin to get a sense of how to show your own product. You should always be mindful of time. It's always good to start with a brief history and performance of the company you represent. You can show some financial ratings along with your company-supplied materials. Now you can begin to introduce your product. You should always treat your product like it's a piece of gold, even if it's just a brochure. You should not just lay a brochure down in front of your prospect. You should present it to him or her, open it up for him or her, and handle it like it's a very fragile piece of glass. If you have a physical product to show, you should present it like it's covered in diamonds, even if it's a construction tool. By doing this, it subliminally illuminates value. You need to arrange your presentation so your prospect continually nods his or her head during your presentation. This is usually accomplished by the logical progression as to how something works. To accomplish all of this, you will really need to practice. You should always be on the lookout for the obvious.

◆ Visual and Verbal Acknowledgements

Visual and verbal acknowledgements are your windows to a sale. When giving a presentation, your prospect will usually give you visual or verbal acknowledgements as you're going along, as in a little nod of the head or just saying "aha." This is an indication that your presentation is moving along swimmingly. At the same time, your prospect may give you a visual concerned expression, as in a smirk or a facial expression that looks like he or she has a question. You certainly don't have to be a body language expert to recognize the obvious. You should be able to recognize these facial expressions instinctively. If you are getting some concerned expressions, you'd better back up and address it immediately. Even though you may have perfected your presentation, you shouldn't become a robot about it. You should always be flexible and attentive to your prospect and ready to react to every concern. In some situations, this can be a real challenge.

◆ The Parkinson's Story (The Most Difficult Sales Presentation Ever Made)

Not so long ago, I was making a presentation to a wonderful lady in her seventies around her kitchen table. I was going about my presentation in the usual way. When we got around to sitting down at her kitchen, it was painfully obvious that she was suffering from Parkinson's disease. Her head shook right to left at a moderate speed. It was an unbelievable challenge to get through that presentation because the visual was a constant no in the movement of her head the entire time. It really threw me off because I'd often stop and ask if she understood. She'd say yes while shaking her head no. I have nothing but empathy for her, but I did find myself humored by my own bewilderment. So visual acknowledgements can sometimes be a challenge.

♦ Bird Story

The verbal part can be interesting as well. Obviously, as you are moving through your presentation and your prospect is verbal, as in saying something, you will respond. I was recently making a presentation my usual way, and it was moving along just fine. As I was deep in the presentation, at the point when I explain the product's most important benefits, this bird comes out of nowhere, flies up on the table, and says "bull<##>." As you can imagine, it was really funny. The bird stayed for the rest of the presentation and pretty much said "bull<##>" intermittently throughout. Even though it was funny, the bird did cause me to be very concerned about its negative input. The prospect's name was Joe. At the end of the presentation, the most amazing thing happened. The bird suddenly said, "It's all bull<##>, Joe." I couldn't believe it. So you should be ready for anything.

♦ Condensed Time Frame

Some of you may say that's just too much time for my product or my prospects. I agree there are times when you don't really have a choice and you must condense your time frame. People can be rushed or have other various reasons. But you won't be able to condense your presentation if you don't have one. You must take the time to prepare and practice and practice your presentation properly. Once you have mastered your product and the delivery of your presentation, then (and only then) you will be able to condense it on the run with authority.

I would have to say my basic presentation for what I do is about five to fifteen minutes. By the time all is said and done with paperwork and everything, it averages around a half hour. But I can condense my presentation down to about five seconds. It goes something like this, "Yes, this is the product you are interested in. It does pretty much everything. Sign here. Any questions? Here's my card. Call me." That really does happen every now and then. It's called a "gimme."

The point here is to be ready. You should not get caught tap dancing. If you do, you will not get anywhere. You can instinctively tell when you need to condense your time frame, perhaps simply because the prospect just doesn't have the time and he or she is hurried or have other reasons. It's sometimes not worth it to condense your presentation that much because of so much valuable information you have prepared to convey. It may be better to try to reset an appointment with that person, but you need to be the judge of that at the time. You would be surprised how many people need to practice this next one.

♦ Your Appearance

Your appearance is number one. Your personal hygiene needs to be in order. You would think I wouldn't even need to bring this up, but some people can offend you so badly that you need to leave the room. You know who you are. If you don't, I will tell you if our paths should ever cross. If you think you might be even close to borderline, step it up a notch. Make sure it will be a pleasure for anyone to be in your company.

Just like hygiene, you would think I wouldn't even need to bring up your appearance when you dress, but some people should have a picture next to the word "slob" in the dictionary. Personally, I do not care to wear a suit. But, because I live in South Florida, it's almost impossible. I like business casual. You need to appear neat, well-dressed, and clean at all times. This is just simply a must.

♦ Your Vehicle

The vehicle you drive has brought about a lot of discussion and opinion over the years. Some say you should have a brand-new or high-end car for business because it gives the appearance that you are successful. The theory is that people are more likely to buy from someone because he or she appears to be successful. Others say it just doesn't matter. The consensus on this issue boils down to two words: decent and respectable. Showing up in a new Mercedes could backfire on you in certain situations; showing up in a hunk of junk could backfire on you in certain situation. It does happen, and you will lose a sale along the way because of it. This is all about your presentation. It does matter. Every little thing matters. You need to mitigate your risk in everything. You just should not do things that may have the chance to work against you. As far as your car is concerned, decent and respectable is the rule of the day, and that will never fail you.

I make a lot of money. For business, I can drive anything I want. For me, the absolute best vehicle for my sales business has been my Ford pickup truck. This may not be the vehicle for you, but it has worked so well for me that this is my fourth one. It works in the poorest parts of town as well as the wealthiest gated communities and everything in between. It is fully equipped with everything you could possibly need to make your sales calls.

On the top left, you can see the navigation system in the dash, a major time-saver. My cell phone, a laptop, and appointment and presentation book are at my fingertips. It's all sitting on top of an auto desk, which you can order online. On the top right, I carry all my brochures and files with me. I can easily access them with the slide-a-bed. You can order one at your local dealer. It's very handy. The bottom left shows a copier on the passenger side floor. You can buy a small power inverter that plugs into the cigarette lighter at Wal-Mart for about fifty bucks. It's very handy. Last but not least, the bottom right is the lunch cooler tucked neatly behind the driver's seat. It's really unbelievable how much time and money this little move makes. I find it hard to top this setup. You can do it up however you like for your needs, but I can tell you for sure that it works.

♦ Attributes

All of these attributes are incorporated in a presentation when you are a professional: finesse, skill, flair, grace, elegance, poise, tact, discretion, assurance, and refinement. In my training experience, I have found that these attributes are difficult, if not at times impossible, to teach for some people. You probably know who I'm talking about. If you haven't acquired at least one or two or three of these at this point in your life, you are probably in the wrong business. These attributes come from deep within a person. They are expressed very differently for each person. The important thing is that you incorporate them in your presentation where appropriate. You should always have them on your mind. Just reviewing the definitions of these attributes will be very helpful. I have taken the liberty to pick the words in the definitions that seem to fit our presentations the best:

- **Attributes:** A quality of character or characteristic
- **Finesse:** Delicacy of execution
- **Skill:** Trained and experienced
- **Flair:** Talent; aptitude; keen perception
- **Grace:** Elegance of beauty of form, manner, motion, or act
- **Respect:** Esteem or deferential regard felt or shown; discrimination or partiality in the regarding of persons or things
- **Elegance:** Gracefully refined, as in tastes or habits; pleasingly superior in quality or act
- **Poise:** A state of balance, steadiness, stability, or composure
- **Tact:** A keen sense of what to say or do to avoid giving offense; a skill in dealing in difficult or delicate situations
- **Discretion:** The power or right of deciding or acting accordingly to one's own judgment
- **Assurance:** A positive declaration, pledge, or guaranty intended to give confidence
- **Refinement:** To bring to a finer state of form to be polished

These things matter a lot, and I know this for a fact. I have often heard prospects describe their salesperson with some of these terms.

What is actually happening here is that you are building customers for life. They like you so much that they won't buy from anyone else.

♦ A Review

There is a lot of work in these first three master keys, but you should be able to see that you can't get to one without the other. You cannot play around with it. It must be done this way. Practice really does make perfect, or at least very close. You should gather all the tools at your disposal to assists you in your presentation. You should do it repeatedly until you are comfortable with a logical rhythm. You should be mindful of your appearance and exercise attributes whenever appropriate.

CHAPTER FIVE

THE FOURTH MASTER KEY: PRESENTATION

You must approach your product presentation with the mind-set and goal that, when you are finished, you are certain that no one could have done it better. The perfect sales presentation is when you have presented yourself and your product so well that the prospect doesn't ask you any questions. He or she just buys it. It does happen, and it happens a lot, almost every day in my case. We have all seen presentations of many things, whether in a group or one-on-one. You can always tell who has done it well and who has not. When you follow this process to your presentation in this book, your presentation will be your autobahn to the point of sale every time, guaranteed.

Many people who have a so-called Type A personality or are gregarious have a natural outgoing personality. Or social butterflies think that, when they present something, they can just wing it and will be just fine. This couldn't be farther from the truth. When you have studied all the master keys, you will be able to separate the professionals from the imposters in a second. It does not matter what kind of personality you have. The master keys to the point of sale will always work for you.

A successful sales presentation is a very serious, well thought out, organized, scientific process. Many things need to be considered and laid out in an orderly fashion. I like the word "fashion" because there is some pizzazz to it. If you are a chef, presentation is everything. It's the finished product. If you know anything about preparing a meal, then you know a lot goes into it. When it's ready, you just can't wait to eat it, and it's a pleasure. Your sales presentation is the same thing. A lot goes into it. When it's done right, your prospect can't wait to buy it with pleasure.

Webster's defines "presentation" as:

- "An act of presenting something or the state of being presented"
- "A performance, exhibition, or demonstration put on before an audience"
- "The manner in which something is shown, expressed, or laid out for other people to see"
- "A formal talk made to a group of people, for example, on somebody's recent work or some aspect of business, often with handouts, diagrams, or other visual aids"
- "An important part of the chef's job"

Looking back on the definition of "presentation," I really like "the manner which something is shown, expressed, or laid out for other people to see." I am a direct salesperson, and I have been for a very long time. My process works the same for individual or a group sale. I am going to walk you through, step-by-step, all the things you must do in your presentation that have been proven to absolutely work every time.

♦ Step One: A Timeline

Lay it out. Lay it all out. It is what it is. Now, with each part of your presentation, we are going to assign a timeline to it. As we go through this, you will clearly see how every moment of your presentation is accounted for. You will also see that every step of your presentation is very controlled and controlled by you. You will have preset every second so you will know what's going to happen in the beginning, the middle, and the end. You have already set much of the timeline for your individual product and practiced it repeatedly. Now we begin to incorporate other master keys and put the presentation together.

♦ Step Two: The Greeting

The very first thing is the greeting. It works the same way in an office as it works in someone's home. You should take five to fifteen minutes to become acquainted. You exchange your hellos and how-do-you-dos. You should always greet your prospect with a firm handshake and give eye contact. Normally then, the prospect will invite you to have a seat. You should always take the seat your prospect leads you to. This is the place in time where the importance of the impressions formed by what was discussed in chapter three matter, and it all happens in a couple seconds.

♦ Trade Secret

Here is a trade secret. If a prospect offers you something to drink, you should always say yes. This is a gesture from the prospect, welcoming you into his or her space. You should next start settling into conversation. You can point out something in the home or office, such as family photos or awards. Perhaps he or she has a little collection of dolls or model cars. Usually, you can always ask about something. Believe me. Your prospect will be happy to tell you all about it. You should always pay attention and compliment as well as you should. This may sound like idle banter, but you should remember that you planned this way ahead of time. You are making a friend. This is the greeting, and we are going to assign the greeting around five to fifteen minutes. The greeting time is very important. This is your time to make a fast friend. The better you do this, the better off you will be. It is said that people don't buy from strangers. They buy from friends. They can buy from anybody, so why should they buy from you? Your time will fluctuate here and there, but you should remember that it is part of your planned presentation as it is assigned a timeline.

♦ Trade Secret

Here's another little trade secret, a subliminal technique called the "mirror technique." When I first was told about this, I thought it was ridiculous until I started using it. The best time to use it is during your greeting time. It works like this. Whatever your prospect is doing, you do the same thing, as if your prospect were looking in a mirror.

- If your prospect is sitting in the chair leaning over to the left with his or her left hand supporting the chin, you do the same thing.

- If the prospect has his or her legs crossed, you cross yours.
- If the prospect has his or her hands folded together, you fold yours together.

The mirror technique makes you appear to the prospect how the prospect appears, thereby creating a comfort zone. The prospect sees you as he or she is himself or herself, thereby subconsciously granting you acceptance into his or her space because you are like he or she is. Now you may think I'm kidding, but this really works every time. When you add your own character and personality to it, you own it. This sets you up to be in the most favorable position to transition to your next step, introducing your product, so make sure you do it. All this happens in the first five to fifteen minutes, but you should remember that you planned it and you were in control of every minute.

♦ Beware of Fern's Disease

As you begin to take control of your greeting time on your timeline, you will always need to be on the lookout for Fern's disease. A Fern sometimes comes along, and there isn't much you can do except ride it out. Fern is a very young, eighty-four-year-old lady. I had the pleasure of selling a product in her home many years ago. I went to her house around ten o'clock in the morning and was not able to get out of there for another nine hours. Keep in mind that I was aware of my five- to fifteen-minute greeting timeline. Fern was one these very charming, little old ladies (and I say that with great affection) who just could not stop talking, but she was a clever old bird. Fern instinctively knew when you were putting on the close, and she would intentionally divert you off your close every time until she was good and ready. Before I knew it, I was sitting at the dining room table, enjoying this wonderful lunch that she had prepared. Fern was talking the entire time, and it became a real challenge to try to find the place when she took a breath because the words kept coming nonstop. The next thing I knew, it was dinnertime. I finally sold her, but I was there for nine hours

A few days later, Fern called the office because she had some questions and wanted me to come back to go over some things. So

I told this story to Harry, and he could not believe it. I did not want to go back over there. I begged Harry to make this service call for me, but he refused. So I said, "Okay, because you don't believe me, I'll give you $100 if you will do this service call." Harry agreed. I said that he could not take more than two hours. Harry thanked me for my generosity and laughed at me.

The same thing happened to Harry. To this day, we still laugh about it.

♦ Step Three: The Product Introduction

The beginning of your presentation should immediately address commonly known objections about your product or industry in a positive manner so you can prevent your prospect from asking about them. We are not talking about overcoming objections at closing time; we are talking about overcoming objections about your product or industry. You should acknowledge mistakes and talk briefly about the new direction your product or industry is going. The Oreck vacuum cleaner is a perfect illustration. The Oreck people overcame the weight problem with vacuum cleaners by being very up front about their machine weighing only eight pounds. They even called it the "eight-pound Oreck." This does two things:

- It overcomes an objection about weight, a product, and industry problem.
- It highlights a value at the same time.

It sure worked on us because we bought one. The presentation of your product must be absolutely convincing. You have the knowledge part down. You have been tested, and you tested yourself. You know what you are talking about. Through that experience, you have gained a significant amount of confidence, but you are not even close to being ready.

♦ Kink-in-the-Armor Syndrome

As you may already know, in sales, somebody wins, and somebody loses. That's very true. Just like in battle, if your opponent finds a weak spot exposed on the battlefield or in your armor, you are dead. The same applies with your sales presentation. If you expose a weak spot in your presentation, you could lose. You should always assume your prospect is as smart as you starting off and always show respect. As your presentation progresses, you will be able to instinctively determine the level of knowledge your prospect has about your product or industry. During that time, you make your adjustments and, as always, with respect. As you begin, you shouldn't worry because your prospects will expose your kinks for you. You will hopefully be able to smooth out your kinks. The kinks don't happen that often because, when one does pop up, you usually won't let it happen again. Once again, the better you are prepared, the faster you will get into production.

♦ My Mother's Car

Back in the early 1980s, my mother wanted to buy a new car. She specifically wanted an economical car, and it had to be red. My father passed away a few years before, and he always joked to my mother how funny it seemed to be that, when the husband died, the first thing the wife did was go out and buy a little red car. So she wanted a little red car. She lived in Pennsylvania. At that time, I was living in Colorado. Naturally, I wanted to help her get the new car and the best deal. At the time, the Honda Prelude was known to be a solid, economical, and reliable car that was reasonably priced. So I was set on that car for her and told her so. She said she was going to look around a little more. A little time went by, so I called to follow up with her to see how her car shopping was going. I was preparing to fly back to Pennsylvania and close the deal for her, like any good son would do. So she told me over the phone that she had gotten sick of looking at cars. She said that she and Uncle Doc (her brother) went out that weekend and bought one.

I said, "Well, okay. What did you get?"
She said, "I forget the name, but I think it's a Chevette."
I said, "A Chevette?"
She said, "Yes, a Chevette."
At the time, the Chevette was about the smallest car made in America. Its wheels were not much bigger than go-cart wheels. Actually, the whole car wasn't much bigger than a go-cart and had less power.
I said, "You got to be kidding me."
She said, "No, I'm not. I thought it was cute."

I said, "Ma, that's the worst car you could have possibly bought in the world."

She said, "It's okay. It's all I need. We think we got a good deal."

I said, "You think you got a good deal?"

She said, "Yes, I do."

I said, "Why didn't you wait for me to come home and help you try to get the best deal?"

I could tell by the hesitation in her voice that she really didn't want to tell me what the real reason was. I kept on probing, so she finally confessed. I couldn't believe it, and it has stuck with me for years. This story is such a classic for presentation and has all the "Keys to Direct Sales Success."

She said, "Well, the salesman was so good. He was so nice and mannerly. He answered all my questions and did everything for me. I just loved him. He was wonderful, so I just had to buy the car from him. I couldn't be more satisfied."

I said, "Really?"

She said, "Really."

I said, "Well, okay, if you are really happy."

She said, "Yes, I'm really happy."

We should all tip our hats to that salesman. I never met him, but whoever he was, he surely was one of the best.

A major part of this practice is to overcome every possible objection you or anyone else can think of throughout your presentation. If you can achieve this, there will be few, if any, questions at all when you have finished. You will need to do this several times. You will need to walk away from it, come back, and do it again. You will find yourself thinking about it in your sleep and often when you wake up. You will have thought of something to add or change. It's the dandiest thing, but it really happens. It's just like the definitions says. You should do it repeatedly in order to improve performance. Once you think you have it down, you now need to present it to someone else, such as co-workers or friends and family. When you do this, you must pay very close attention to their responses, questions, and body language. By paying attention to these details, you can easily tell if you have presented your product smoothly. You should make your adjustments where appropriate. Remember that your presentations will never be identical, but they will be close.

♦ The Wooing Factor

Just the other day, after I had finished with a sale, I had some time to kill so I was sitting and talking to this very nice lady about this book, which I was writing at the time. I was telling her about the outline of the book and all the steps.

Then she said "And the wooing factor?"

I said, "What?"

She said, "Yes, the wooing factor."

I had never heard that one before, so I asked, "What do you mean?"

She said my presentation was like a romantic dance. It was a very pleasant experience, and I enjoyed you a lot. I really didn't need your product, but I wanted to buy it from you anyway. Thus, this is the "wooing factor." To me, this explained my mother's car story. There is a lot of power in a smile.

♦ A Review

You must approach your product presentation with the mind-set and goal that, when you are finished, you are certain that no one could have done it better. All of this is accomplished with these master keys in this order:

- Practice, practice, practice.
- Lay it all out. Give everything a timeline.
- Streamline.
- Work on the nuances of your greeting.
- Keep the trade secrets in mind.
- Transition to your product presentation by continually overcoming objections from the very beginning to the end.

CHAPTER SIX

THE FIFTH MASTER KEY: PERPETUAL CLOSE

Webster's defines "perpetual" as:
- "Continuing for an unlimited period of time"
- "Continuous"

Throughout your sales career, you will attend many sales meetings. Many of them will be about closing the deal. You will hear a gazillion ways to overcome an objection and close a sale. Most will be goofier than the goofiest. I think I have heard them all, and I listened because I really wanted it to all tie in and make sense. After all these years, it has become very clear that you are in a state of closing from the time you open your mouth to your prospect to the time your prospect signs the bottom line. Thus, this is the "perpetual close."

Preparing yourself and adhering to the sales master keys in this book is the only way. A gazillion closes are already built into these master keys. This sales process of your entire sales presentation works because you created the presentation specifically to overcome any objections. It will work for you every time. Once you start doing your presentation several times, it will all fall into place. It's magical and works most of the time. I have probably done my product presentation literally thousands of times. Because I'm so well-rehearsed, my perpetual closing presentation morphs into an assumptive closing presentation. The assumptive close technique simply means your attitude during your presentation is that you just assume your prospect is going to buy from you because it works beautifully. Out of all the closes in the world, I have only had to use one other one on occasion. Don't get me wrong. I have always been very open to using any other closes or closing technique out there. But I have found this sales process eliminates most of them. Once again, it's because I prepared it that way. The only other close I sometime use is the repeat close.

◆ Repeat Close

Even though your prospect acknowledged that he or she understood everything throughout your presentation, he or she sometimes doesn't. You can readily tell by the questions he or she asks that he or she didn't get it. Sometimes, the nuances of some products can be a little tricky, so it's very important to go over it again until your prospect thoroughly gets it. You can usually instinctively tell when your prospect doesn't understand something. You can see it in his or her facial expressions. Sometimes, you just need to ask him or her if there is something you need to go over again. Thus, this is the "repeat close."

If you are using too many closes at the end of your presentation, you need to redo your presentation and incorporate those objections into your new presentation

◆ Point of Sale

The point of sale is a particular moment or stage in a process, especially one at which a significant change or development occurs. We have reached the point at which a decision will have to be made. And here we are. This is what we live for. This is where you need to be. This is where you make your money. All that you have learned and all your preparation comes down to this moment. So what do you do now? You shut up.

That's right. You should shut up. It is often said in a sale that someone wins and someone loses. At this point, the contest is decided. It is also said that the first one who speaks will lose. These are both true. Everything comes down to that very moment where there is nothing more to say. You must stop talking, say nothing, and wait. You should shut up. The first one who speaks will lose.

You must discipline yourself and adhere to this time-tested closing rule. It's true, and it works. You should never ever forget it.

It can feel like a long time has passed. Even so, you must zip it. You shouldn't say a word. Your prospect will eventually speak. When he or she does, you won.

This may very well be the most important lessons in sales that you will ever learn. It can really be hard to do at times, that is, to just stop talking, but you must. You should practice it repeatedly with family, friends, or business associates until it's so imbedded in you that it becomes your nature and is routine for you. When you are at the point of sale, you should force yourself to shut up. You will be sure to be a winner playing this numbers game.

♦ A Review

The perpetual close is a part of the presentation, but it so important to the sale that it is a master key on its own. In reality, you are in a state of closing from the time you start until the time you finish. The goal is to do your presentation and overcome all objections so well that your prospect has no questions but where to sign.

CHAPTER SEVEN

THE SIXTH MASTER KEY: DISCIPLINE

Webster's defines "discipline" as:

- "Training to act in accordance with rules, drill, or military discipline"
- "The practice or methods of teaching and enforcing acceptable patterns of behavior"
- "A controlled orderly state, especially in a class of schoolchildren"
- "The ability to behave in a controlled and calm way, even in a difficult or stressful situation"
- "Mental self-control used in directing or changing behavior, learning something, or training for something"

All the definitions are good, but I really like the second one. It's like enforcing patterns of behavior on yourself. For some very good salespeople, clearly, the most difficult discipline in our business is just getting out of bed. Next is getting out of the house. I was going to say, "Get up and go," but just getting up is very difficult all by itself. To then get ready and get out of the house is another thing all together. All too often, a salesperson will start off and do really great in the beginning, make a lot of money, and then suddenly get so lazy.

◆ Get Out of Bed

In the beginning, you should try as best you can to get out of bed before noon. When you have accomplished that comfortably, you should try moving up your wake-up time by fifteen-minute increments. Remember that you don't want to get up too early at first because it might be a shock to your system. Then you will be miserable all day. Once you have gone through this process for a period of time and are now able to get up around ten o'clock, you should take a break so you can see what's going on in the world around that time. When you come back from your vacation, you should pick back up on the process again until you can get to nine o'clock and then ultimately eight o'clock. I know this can be very difficult and you may not be able to do it at first, but you should be persistent and take it slowly. You will get there. If you fall back on your goal, it is perfectly okay to sleep late on the weekends when necessary. Eight o'clock in the morning will be a good time for you to get up.

♦ Get Out of the House

Once you have your goal of eight o'clock, you can now begin to work on getting out of the house. Now that you are able to get up around eight o'clock, you should give yourself plenty of time to get ready. In the beginning, I recommend around four hours. Remember that we don't want to shock your system too much in the beginning. You should take a long shower, enjoy a leisurely breakfast, look around, and, once again, see what's going on around at that time in the morning.

Once you have your routine established, you should begin trying to do your routine just a little faster, but you should not go too fast because we do not want you to get frustrated during the exercise. Once again, you should try taking off fifteen minutes at a time. You should keep doing this until you think you can be out of the house, in your car, and on your way by nine o'clock. When you are getting close to your goal of nine o'clock, you should stop and take another short vacation. The vacation is important. You need to reward yourself and take a break from all the stress and strain you put yourself through. Once you have mastered the two most difficult and challenging sales disciplines, you can now set your sights on sales success. These two disciplines can arguably account for 100 percent of your sales. Simply put, "If you ain't there, nothing happens!"

If you do your prospecting by appointment, as I do, a really good routine is getting up at eight o'clock and getting out by nine o'clock. You should set four appointments by whatever way you do your marketing. You should set one appointment at ten o'clock, noon, two o'clock, and four o'clock. That's it. It sounds simple, and it is. You just have to work at it and make it happen.

The most critical aspect of getting up and going is, "Even if you have no place to go, just go anyway!" Someone once said, "If you just go, there's so much business out there that you'll trip over it." It's true.

♦ A Routine

You should establish a routine every day. Aside from all of these critical keys to direct selling success, this one is a biggie. One of the biggest reasons I have outperformed my peers consistently over the years is simply because I do it and I do it every day.

♦ Time Management

When you get to the point where you have these basic disciplines a little under control, you should make a concerted effort toward time management. Time is money, and there is a lot of truth to it. The better you manage your time, the more opportunities you will have to make money. Years ago, I attended courses that the Day-Timer company gave. They specialize in time management and time management tools. Now they can show you how to manage every minute of your day, but you don't need to go that far. But many of these tips will most certainly prove to be very helpful.

Many things in your life need to be somewhat organized in order for you to perform well or at all. Today, many tools will help you manage your time better, from a regular calendar to computer notebooks, desktops, and even cell phones. You should check them all out and find the one that best fits your needs. So while you're busy managing your time, you should make sure you manage some time for yourself and your family. When you write down some time for yourself in your schedule, it looks good just being there, and it is certainly something to look forward to.

♦ Be On Time

The definition of being on time for anything is fifteen minutes early. This discipline is critical in every appointment situation. In every case scenario, it will be better for you if you show up at least fifteen minutes early rather than be one minute late. It doesn't mean the appointment will start early. It just means you are ready and have a little time to gather yourself. A long time ago, I spent six years in the United States Army Infantry on active duty. The infantry are the foot soldiers (or "grunts" or "bush beaters"). They walk and run everywhere. They are very happy when they get a ride. During that time, the battalion, brigade, or even division would occasionally have a competition to be the commander's driver. It was a coveted and prestigious position for many reasons, but mostly, you'd be riding. This was not an easy competition to say the least. You basically had to be the best soldier at each of those levels to win that job. The competition was grueling. You went before a board of sergeant majors at every level. You had to know every detail about your job and be in top physical condition to pass many physically challenging courses. You needed to look and act at the highest military level. Your boots needed to look like glass. You had to pass numerous inspections of every kind. If you had a piece of lint on your uniform, you could be eliminated. The stakes were high because they wanted to put forth their best soldier for the commander.

I went for those jobs and got them. I drove for commanders at every level of the military to the top. I spent five years as the general's driver. It was really something. I drove for many generals over those years. The Secret Service even selected me to drive for the president when he visited the military base.

Driving with the Secret service

Meeting President Jimmy Carter

Gen. PX Kelly   *Maj. Gen. Marianne Chapman*

Gen. John Vessey   *Lt. Gen David Grange*   *BG. JW Nicholson*

Maj. Gen RC Kingston   *Seaman Bud Manley*   *Sergeant Mike Manley*

"Combat Football"

I shared this story with you because I want to get back to the importance of being on time. It applies to every place you need to be at an appointed time. Can you imagine being the driver for some of the most powerful people in our country and being late? I can, and it won't happen too many times!

◆ Play the Numbers

The numbers game is basically, "The more opportunities you have to sell, the more you will sell." There is absolutely no question that, if you play the numbers, you will win every time. The problem with the numbers game is the discipline to just keep doing it and never get discouraged. Professional sports are a great example. Most professional sport teams play every week for the most part, but they don't win every week. But they're back out there, week after week, giving it their best shot all year long. They do eventually win. They are discouraged when they are in a slump, but they keep at it.

You just have to know for absolute certainty that it will work in your favor. The more times you are up to bat, the better your chances of hitting the ball. It's just that simple. It really can be hard sometimes. It can take some time. You will run into a dry spell, but only every now and then. In every case, over a period of measured time, you will surpass your own expectations. That's easy to say, but in direct sales, there are ways to do this.

◆ Prospecting

Prospecting is the act of looking forward in time or anticipating. If you are selling anything, you are prospecting. Who wants to buy my product? Who needs to buy my product? How do I find these people? How do these people find me? Major companies prospect by using TV, radio, and print adds. For a direct salesperson, it's different because you are zeroing in your prospect as opposed to broad general advertising. The way you prospect is in direct relationship to the product you want to sell. I use three types of prospecting: telemarketing, mailers, and referrals.

◆ Telemarketing

Telemarketing can be irritating and is somewhat controversial across the nation. Many new laws apply to the telemarketing industry these days, such as the National Do Not Call Registry and registering to even buy a list to call. On a local area basis, it seems to work quite well. Several companies will provide you with lists to call, and they can customize your lists to target your prospect. They can break down the list by age, income, zip code, area code, and so forth. I think they are reasonably priced with incentives for you to come back to buy additional lists. The problem is finding a good telemarketer. The best way I have found is to run an ad in the newspaper. You will get a good response. You just have to interview them and go with the best one you think will work best for you. You will sometimes have to go through a few before you get the right one, but when you find one, you'd better pay them well with incentives. I have found it best to pay them a base salary per week or month and a bonus per sale. You shouldn't give them a hard time. You should always be as nice as you can be. You should never shortchange them. When in doubt, you should pay them. If they are sick, you should pay them. If they need a day off, you should pay them. When you take a vacation, you should pay them. A good one is hard to find. You need to take care of them. It will pay off in the long run.

♦ Mailers

A steady recurring mailer with a return response card has always worked well for me. You need to work it a little, dropping different zip codes at different times. A drop will usually cost you one or maybe two commissions of a sale, but in the worst case, if you only get five or ten responses, you are still way ahead of the game. In most cases, you will get a lot more. Of course, the mailer is in direct scale to your production, but once you get it going, the more you can do. Telemarketing and a mailer is a great combination for a direct salesperson.

♦ Referrals

Every sales organization will pound this one into you. Some of them want you to get so deep into it that it becomes irritating and uncomfortable for you and your prospect. With direct sales, I have found that, when you have completed your sale, the very last thing is to just ask for a referral. You should just ask, "Do you know anyone who may need my product or service?" It's really just that simple. If you have done everything right, your costumer will always be happy to refer you. The hardest part is sometimes remembering to ask. You should always ask and leave an extra business card for your prospect to pass on.

Once you start your job and follow the keys in this book, you should buy a really nice car. The more expensive, the better. You will never find a successful salesperson driving a clunker. You wanted to know how to acquire the discipline to run the numbers to get your sales on a daily basis. Now you have to make that car payment. You could get married and have a kid or two. Believe me, you will be out there every day. I don't think you're going to have any difficulty finding reasons why you need money and why you need to be out there making sales. You just can never get discouraged and just know that playing the numbers will always reward you.

As I look back, I did get discouraged. I did have a tough time in the beginning until I started to listen and learn from successful people who came before me. I hated it when I missed a sale. It would make me crazy trying to figure out what I was doing wrong. I really didn't believe in the numbers and the process of selling as I do now. Someone once told me that, when you have done everything you possibly could, as in following the master keys in this book, and you don't get the sale, you should be happy. It just simply means the next one is waiting to buy from you so you need to get going because he or she is waiting for you. It's so true.

No one closes a sale every single time, but the one who follows the master keys and believes in the numbers and prospecting just does it more than most. It took me a while, but I'm happy if I miss a sale. I can't wait to get to my next appointment. I know my product, and I know the process. I am prepared, but most of all, before I am done with my prospect, I always pause for a moment and ask myself, "Is there anyone I know who could have done it better than me?" When I feel certain no one could come in behind me and make that sale, at that point (and only at that point), I'm happy to move on.

You should be confident in this knowledge and know it is fact. No one team wins every game, but that doesn't mean they didn't play well. No one golfer gets a par at every hole, but that doesn't mean he or she is not a great golfer. No one race car driver wins every race, even though he or she is a great driver. No one singer gets a number-one hit every time he or she records a song, even if the song is great. No one actor or actress gets an Oscar every time he or she appears in a movie, but that doesn't mean he or she didn't give a great performance. Just because you didn't get the gold medal, that doesn't mean you can't.

As you can see, we are all playing the numbers game. The more we play, the better we get. Most of all, you should always remember, "If you don't play, you can't win." So:

- Get up.
- Get out of the house.
- Prospect and get your appointments.
- Play the numbers and play every day.

♦ Avoid Obstacles to the Point Of Sale

The point of sale is where you make your money, so that's where you need to be. Over the years, I have observed many people in the sales industry who seem to be doing everything else except what they should be doing. It's really amazing how many things seem to come up and just get in the way of you even making an opportunity exist to even give yourself a chance to be at the point of sale. It just so happens that's the place where you make your living.

This subject is the primary reason I thought about writing this book. Even today, I outproduce most sales agents in the country. When we gather for meetings, many salespeople come up to me because they know my numbers. They ask, "How do you do that?" My first quick answer is always, "I just get out there and do it." That's 90 percent of the battle. I give everything else in this book about 10 percent, but that 10 percent is an absolute must. It's indisputable, and you cannot argue with it at all. You just must know it. That's the end of that story. It doesn't really matter how much you know or practice. If you don't get out and do it and hone those skills, you are just wasting your time.

♦ Excuses

Probably the biggest obstacle of all is the excuses, the sometimes never-ending excuses and mostly lame excuses. All those reasons are why you say you couldn't be where you should have been. I am sure there is a book about excuses that has yet to be written. Some of you reading this book could probably write it. Some excuses are naturally acceptable, like emergencies, but with salespeople, even those excuses are questionable.

Excuses are obstacles to the point of sale, and that's a fact. When you're thinking of your next excuse, you really need to try really hard to remember what you're reading here. Stop and ask yourself in all sincerity, "Is this an excuse? Who am I kidding?" You will typically find that you are only kidding yourself to your own detriment.

I did have one of my agents come up with a pretty good excuse one time. She said she missed her appointment because she was abducted. At first, I showed concern. I thought she might be having some kind of serious domestic problems. No, she said aliens had abducted her. I just simply said okay and left it at that. I was right about one thing. She was having some serious problems.

◆ Avoid Obstacles to the Point Of Sale

You really need to sit down and take the time to think about what you do during the course of the day. What obstructs you from what you should be doing? You need to identify the obstacles and think about what they are costing you. When you have recognized an obstacle in your life, you should take the time to write it down. It doesn't matter if it's a really little one or a really big one. You write it down as a confirmed obstacle because this is a conscious act. The next time that obstacle confirmed by you appears, your subconscious will automatically kick in and remind you what it is. It's the dandiest thing, but it works. Soon, you will recognize what needs to be cleared out of the way for you to better produce.

◆ Obstacles Are Choices

Obstacles can be choices. In other words, you choose to drink a gallon of coffee and watch TV before you do anything. Maybe you could drink a half a gallon of coffee, record the TV program, and watch it later. I like to stop in on car dealerships and see what's new during my workday. At times, I have spent a lot of time just shooting the breeze, knowing I'm not going to buy anything. I am clearly wasting productive time during my workday. I made a choice not to do that anymore during my workday, but only do it after hours or on the weekends. Every time I drive by a car dealership now during my workday, I am subconsciously reminded of the decision I made not to do it during the workday, and I drive on by. I have a telemarketer who sets my appointments daily. A good day would be an appointment at ten, noon, two, and four. You can't always get four appointments a day. That's just the nature of the business. She usually calls them in for me the night before and leaves them on my recorder. I usually retrieve them in the morning. She sometimes won't have a ten or a noon appointment for me. There have been times where we blanked all day, but it's very seldom. Ah, those times are great. I can stay out late, sleep in, chill out, or maybe plan something else fun and relaxing to do. I just love my job, the good life. The problem is that's not what happens here. What happens is I get up and go anyway. I go to the area in which I'm working and find a place to park, like a park, a mall, or some other parking area. I'll just sit there and wait until she finds me an appointment to go to. That's the difference and a great illustration of avoiding an obstacle to the point of sale. The obstacle in this case is me staying at home. So, if I slept in, she'd think, "Ah, he's sleeping in. I don't want to bother him, so I won't even try to set an appointment for him this morning." However, now that she knows I'm waiting out there somewhere, it changes the entire dynamic. She tries harder than ever to get me an appointment and usually does.

Going out to lunch is one of the biggest obstacles to the point of sale there is and a waste of valuable time. Now I know some of you will say, "Oh, I conduct business over lunch." Well, only if that is really true. Probably not. But certainly not the case if you are a prospecting direct salesperson. Going out to lunch with someone can take up to two hours out of your day. Going out to lunch with someone is just an excuse for you to get out of what you should be doing. You can take a break when you die.

I take my lunch and drinks with me when I go. I take a sandwich wrapped in cellophane. I take some soda with me in a cooler. The cost per unit or can is around twenty-five cents. I make really good money, so don't think I'm just being cheep. I've been to more of these time-wasting lunches than I care to remember. But I must say that the savings are astounding and the time saved is invaluable. Most of the time, I will eat my sandwich while I'm driving and sipping my soda that I keep placed neatly in its cup holder. I'm not trying to suggest anything unsafe. I'm just telling you what I do. I'm usually done with my lunch in about five minutes. The times goes by so fast that it's like it didn't even happen. I do this every day. It's a routine for me.

◆ Costly Obstacles

As a direct salesperson, not getting up and out under any circumstances was a costly obstacle to the point of sale. As a direct salesperson, going out to lunch was a costly obstacle to the point of sale. All I needed to do was look at my productivity and commission check before and after making these changes. Now, because I avoid just these two obstacles to the point of sale, my income has increased by more than $100,000.

♦ A Review

All the master keys are a must and very important, but this one will put you on the leaderboard and keep you there. I am certain that this is why I usually outperform most all other salespeople. I do it. I really practice what I preach. I will be the first to admit that it's not always easy, but you just have to keep at it. I am sure there are many things in your individual personal lives that you need to do so you can get out there and really produce. As long as you are aware of these things and they always pop up, you can start to begin a productive, disciplined routine and continue to refine it.

CHAPTER EIGHT

THE SEVENTH MASTER KEY: FOLLOW SUCCESS

Mike Manley receives the Aflac coveted Amos Award (center) from Chairman and CEO Dan Amos (left) and Founder John Amos (right). The Amos Award is given to the top agent in USA. Mike also receives awards for a lifetime membership in the prestigious Presidents Club.(photo right & left)

Your manager doesn't really like you hanging around the office. Even though his or her smile is courteous and helpful at times, he or she may not even like you at all. He or she is not going to pay your mortgage, rent, or car payment. Even if he or she did (and I have known some who would), he or she won't do it for long.

You need to associate yourself with the people who are doing the deal. You should seek out the people who are on the leaderboard. These people consistently produce without supervision, day in and day out. You should talk to them, find out what they are doing, and figure out how they do what they do. You should listen and pick up on the tips they will give you. They will be more than happy to tell you what they do and how great they are. You should take some time to read about some real success stories in history and success stories happening in America today. There are many, and they are rich with moral and virtue. Walt Disney's father yelled at him one day for drawing mice in the back of their garage. His father said, "Walt, quit drawing those mice and get a real job!" We all know the rest of that story. Charlie Watts, the drummer for the Rolling Stones, once said, "When I first joined the band in June, I was praying to God that we would make it through the summer." We all know the rest of that story as well. Michael Flatley of Riverdance and Lord of the Dance fame took an old country Irish jig and made a billion dollars.

It wasn't that long ago that I was the number-one agent in the state for my product when I lived in Colorado. Harry brought to my attention that I was simultaneously competing for the number-one spot nationally. I started paying really close attention to that national leaderboard and haven't looked back. One other fellow was always right there in the running. The lead went back and forth and back and forth. This went on for months. I was losing sleep over this competition, and I didn't even know this guy. He wound up being L. Douglas Greer, an agent from Columbus, Georgia. I won a trip to visit the Aflac home office. I didn't really care that much about visiting the home office, even though it's a great place. I was very excited to go to Columbus, Georgia, so I could meet Doug. I was just dying to know what he was all about. I met Doug, and we became fast and lifelong friends. That year, I became the number-one agent in the United States, but to this day, I'm not so sure I could have beat Doug. Doug recruited me from Colorado to Columbus. Doug then took a promotion to district manager. I wound up being in Doug's district and his top agent. Doug wound up being the number-one district in the country. Now isn't that just something. I have to tell you that we had the time of our life.

♦ Do the Right Thing

In most sale organizations, there are always rules, laws, and regulations that we all need to follow. For many of us, there is always licensing, updates, and continuing education that seem never-ending. As if that isn't enough, your company will usually have additional endless meetings with respect to compliance and how to represent and conduct yourself in the field or anytime you're representing the company. With all the stuff they throw at you, it really boils down to just one thing, doing the right thing.

When I'm giving this presentation, I'm often asked, "How do I know what the right thing is?" It is a good question, and it deserves a good answer. You only need to remember three things:

- As human beings, we just instinctively know the difference between right and wrong. It's a God-given sense. You feel it, and you just know it. At this stage of your life, you should already know this.
- In the mid-1980s, I was at a conference with Aflac. The then-president and now-chairman and CEO, Dan Amos, was speaking. I don't remember everything about that speech that day, but I do remember him addressing this subject about doing the right thing. He said, "When representing our company, represent our company as if I were there with you." If you know anything about Dan Amos, you knew you heard that from a man who has probably been the most respected and accomplished CEO in our country for decades. He really is a man of impeccable integrity and honor. I only say that because I know it firsthand to be true.
- Over the years, many really Christian folks have told me, "The devil has no authority over me." Now that pretty much says it all, and it really stuck.

Even today, when I find myself in a potential sticky situation (and it happens to all of us), I always remember my own human instincts, what Dan Amos said, and the quote from the Christian folk, and I always act accordingly. I have never had a complaint in twenty-seven years. These three answers to that question have served me well over many years, and they will for you as well.

Hopefully, you have a CEO of such character. They are hard

to come by these days. The best thing about doing the right thing always is that you will always feel good about what you do. More importantly, you will feel good about yourself.

◆ Enthusiasm

Webster's defines "enthusiasm" as "passionate interest in or eagerness to do something." This says it all. When you have the knowledge and you have practiced, you will become confident. When you have worked on all the master keys, you will see the light at the end of the tunnel, and there will be a bright light for your future in sales. You will know what to do and how to do it. When all this happens, you will also become enthusiastic about what you do. It may be difficult to shut you up. Enthusiasm is magical because it's contagious. Even the people around you will be affected in a positive and motivating way.

Many things and people in this life will challenge or compromise our enthusiasm, sometimes on a daily basis. It can be hard at times when this happens, and it can happen in many different ways. It can be an industry problem. It can be company downsizing or layoffs. It can be things you have no control over or nothing to do with. Many times, it is personal matters. Many other things can happen that can put a damper on your enthusiasm. The best way to protect yourself against these types of things from happening is to expect them. You should try to think of everything and everyone that could or would put a damper on your enthusiasm for whatever reason and expect it to happen. You should think ahead, anticipate it, expect it, prepare yourself for your response or reaction, and be ready. The better prepared you are for these types of things and these type of people, the less likely anything or anyone can knock you down. In fact, when you anticipated someone challenging or compromising your enthusiasm and have planned an enthusiastic response, you will have a positive effect on them as well. Enthusiasm is contagious.

◆ The V-ha Online Story

In the late 1990s, I was at the top of my game with respect to landing very large accounts for employee benefits. Most were national; some were international. But the efficiency of the enrollment process with multiple locations was a nightmare. At the time, no one could do it with any level of efficiently whatsoever. At the dawn of the Internet, I wondered if it would be possible to do all of this over the World Wide Web. At the time I looked and researched everywhere, I could, and no one was doing this. Everyone I talked to about this concept agreed with me that it was a great idea. I developed the outline for the software to make this a reality. But this would be a very expensive undertaking. I always made good money, but I didn't have this kind of money. It would take millions to develop. I made an appointment at my local Merrill Lynch office, went there, and made my presentation, and they loved it. Next thing you know, the company is formed, and I'm running around the country raising money. I raised millions. I'm suddenly Mr. Big and worth millions on paper.

As far as the software development, I knew what it needed to do, but as far as the complexities of a stock company preparing to go public with the Wall Street boys, I was in over my head, and I knew it. In order to protect my interest, I hired a couple of high-end, well-connected lawyers from Washington DC. I paid them handsomely with major stock incentives. While they prepared the company to go public, I traveled the country, demonstrating the technology and landing every account. Things couldn't have been looking better. I even met with United States congressmen who saw it as a vision for the future that would help America run more efficiently.

Finally, the day came when we could test the technology on a real group of employees, and it worked. We were the first company to ever do this. I felt like a hero. It was one of the greatest days of my life. Shortly thereafter, the very people I personally selected to sit on my board, who I trusted and paid very well, kicked me out of my own company. I knew something like this was possible, so I did everything I could to protect myself against it, but it happened anyway. I couldn't believe it.

Looking back, I just didn't realize the level of greed and ruthless nature of lawyers. To this day, I have never met a lawyer who didn't posses these qualities. I was surprised, however, by one investor who was actually worse than a lawyer was. A short time after I was gone, he managed to manipulate and gain control of the company. He forced the company in a direction away from its original mandate, against everyone's interest. His direction was for his own self-interest. He and his team were ruthless with a smile. Ultimately, he drove the company to collapse and then into bankruptcy. He caused many good people to lose a lot of money. The surprise is that he was a pastor of a very large congregation.

I included a copy of the brochure we used. It looked really great and worked really well. Check it out. Today, many insurance companies have and use this technology, but I had it first, and it got away. Apparently, stories like this are more common than you would think. What an experience this was. Talk about enthusiasm or the lack thereof, or talk about getting back up after being slammed to the ground. We can talk.

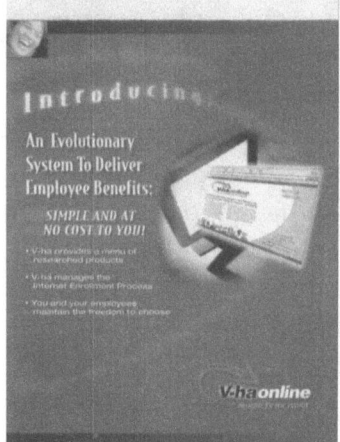
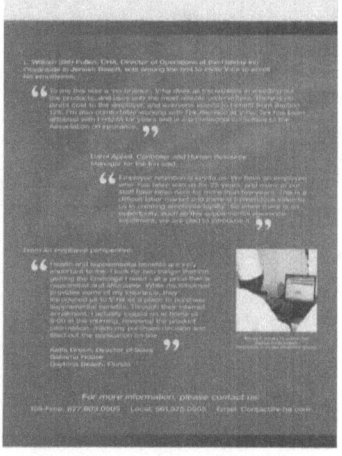
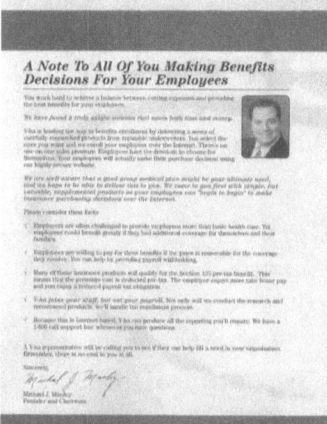

◆ The Fireball

When you first begin and just come out of your training, they usually get you all pumped up, and you are ready to go. And most of you will. I have seen this happen so many times when a salesperson will be all fired up and then suddenly or slowly burn out. I think it's unreasonable to think that anyone in sales can stay on fire all the time, but I do think it's reasonable that you can stay hot. Staying hot is the key. The goal is to transition most of your fireball activities into your daily routine. There should be no reason why you can't at least stay hot once you get on fire.

Everyone in sales has had some success, or he or she wouldn't keep doing it. Anyone trying to get into sales thinks he or she can be successful as well, or he or she wouldn't try. So why is there the turnover? Why does the fire fade? This is why I am so insistent on how you do things in your sales process because it does matter. Now that you clearly know what to do in a proper direct sales process, you will notice the shortcomings of salespeople you encounter. You will feel sorry for them. You will say to yourself, "Forgive them, Lord, for they know not what they do." When you follow the process in this book, you will become a fireball for sure. So the big question is, "How do I stay on fire?"

A good friend and sales associate of mine called me just last night. He calls me frequently just to see how many sales I have for the week or the month. He is a great sales competitor as well. I had about fifty sales over a two-week period. That's pretty hot. He had about one hundred and fifty for the same two weeks. Now that's a fireball. He called me just to try to rub it in. He said, "Yeah, man, I've been unbelievably busy. It's too much. I can't wait for April so I can quit." Sounds like a fireball about to burn out, doesn't it? He tried to rub it in because he knows I am a proven consistent producer. By the year's end, I will wind up smoking him.

It's unrealistic to think you can stay on fire, but it's very realistic that you can stay hot. The key to this transition is to know your burn rate, and you know what that is for yourself. You can feel it coming on. When you feel it coming on, you should pull back, but never quit keep going. At that point, you will be able to realize what a good level of consistent, competitive production is for you. My definition of competitive production is "your name is always on the leaderboard." Now don't get that confused with the comfort zone. That's where salespeople only produce just enough to get by. For some people, it's not much. What we're talking about here is performing at the maximum level that you're able to do consistently so it keeps you on the leaderboard.

♦ People Just Love To Be Sold

Just think about yourself. I know I love to be sold. It's a great feeling. I have a great appreciation and respect for a salesperson who has done everything just so perfectly that I couldn't wait to buy. I couldn't be happier that I bought that product from that person. Just ask my mother about her Chevette. When that happens to me, two words come to mind, "I'm impressed." It takes a lot to impress me, but it takes a lot to impress most of us. We all appreciate a job well done, no matter what it is. When you get to be that good and your prospect is impressed and happy he or she bought from you, you're on your way.

♦ A Review

As you follow these master keys and you get going and start experiencing some success, you will automatically gravitate to those who are successful in the business that you do. You are going to want to get to know them, so do it. They will keep you enthused. I really don't think you will have any trouble with doing the right thing because, as you get older, you can't seem to remember yesterday. People who cheat and lie need to remember everything. They are caught because they can't remember. By doing the right thing all the time, you don't ever need to worry about all of that. Thousands of people are always waiting to see you, so go see them. Don't waste your time with a potential problem. Just stay on fire.

CHAPTER NINE

THE EIGHTH MASTER KEY: HAVE FUN

Harry Hedges, Aflac Chairman & CEO
Dan Amos and Mike Manley In Hawaii.

Aflac Founder John Amos and
Mike Manley In Hawaii

I don't need to write much about this chapter because you already know how to do that. However, in all my years of doing this, I don't know of anyone who has had as much fun as I have. I hope I can meet you one day and you can tell me differently. I look forward to that conversation. Maybe over lunch? I added a few interesting sales stories I encountered along the way.

◆ Be Prepared to Sing

This has happened to me on more than one occasion. I would go to somebody's house on an appointment, knock, be greeted, and enter, only to immediately notice a musical instrument proudly displayed. In this case, it was an organ, easy enough to start my greeting time conversation about. I asked this very nice lady about the organ. She wanted to tell me all about it. It really was a very nice organ. She said it cost over $100,000, and it looked it. She was more than eager to play it for me, so she started it up. She told me this organ had a computer system that could accompany her, playing just about every song that was ever recorded. So she asked what song I would like to hear. I really didn't know, but I said "Summer Wind" by Frank Sinatra. She plugged the song into the computer, and then it started up. It sounded like I was at a live show in Las Vegas with a full orchestra. The organ also had a karaoke screen so you could also sing along. The music started. She handed me the microphone. The next thing you know, I was singing "Summer Wind." Actually, I think I'm pretty good, and it was a lot of fun. Talk about breaking the ice. Keep in mind that I just got in the house. It just doesn't get any better than this to transition to your sales presentation on a positive note.

♦ Be Prepare To Be Entertained

On a similar note, I went to another appointment. I knocked, and I was greeted. I entered the home, only to see five ukuleles proudly displayed. Naturally, I once again started my greeting time by asking about the ukuleles. He was more than eager to tell me all about them. Not only that, as you might expect, he had to play for me as well. Not only did he have to play, he had to sing as well. This was not just singing. This was yodeling. As you might expect, it wasn't long before I started yodeling as well. Once again, I just got in the house. It just doesn't get any better than this to transition to your sales presentation on a positive note. These things really do happen.

♦ The Most Incredible Story Ever Told

One routine, bright, sunny morning, I headed out on my first appointment. As I entered the home, a very nice, older lady welcomed and greeted me. I did all the usual greeting time up to that point. She guided me into the kitchen to sit down along with her husband. He didn't greet me at all.

I sat down at the table and exchanged pleasantries. The woman was very responsive, but the man ignored me totally. Even his eyes looked downward. At any rate, I proceeded with my presentation. The lady continued to be very receptive. The man continued to ignore me as if he wished I weren't even there. He gave me the feeling of the definition of rudeness to the tee. Undaunted, I continued my presentation in the most positive and enthusiastic way. Suddenly, the man just stood up, left the room, and headed down the hallway toward his bedroom. Undaunted, once again, I just continued the presentation with his wife. About midway through, she asked if I would mind her checking on him. I said, "Please do." She hollered down the hall for him. There was no answer, so I continued. After a moment or two, she hollered for him again. There was still no answer. We continued once again for a few moments. She then yelled for him a third time. There was still no answer.

At that point, she left the table and went back to check on him. Suddenly, I heard her screaming and crying as she headed back up the hallway. She said, "My husband is dead!"

There I was, sitting at the kitchen table. She came down the hall crying with her hands over her eyes. I thought, "What to do?" I thought I should call 9-1-1 and maybe some family members to help her out. As she was walking toward the kitchen, in her grief, she tripped over the divider between the hallway carpeting and kitchen floor tile. She fell onto the kitchen floor tile and was knocked unconscious. I could

71

immediately see a golf ball-sized welt forming on her head. Suddenly, the world stopped for me. There I was, sitting at the table with her husband dead in the bedroom and she unconscious on kitchen floor. I was thinking, "Who is going to believe this?"

I thought that, if the police came, they'd never believe this story. I'd be off to prison for the rest of my life. It was surely a career-ending appointment. I was struggling to do the right thing, but at the same time, I knew this wasn't going to work. All I did was go to an appointment and sit at the kitchen table. No one who walked in at this point could ever believe my innocence. Suddenly, a miracle happened. The wife came to. She was only out about a minute, the longest minute of my life to date.

After she gained her composure, we called 9-1-1. They, along with the police, came. When the police came, I could tell they were immediately suspicious of me. The whole scene looked bad. Even though the wife explained everything exactly as it happened, the police still interrogated me for eight hours. You are guilty until proven innocent. This is a true story, but it is truly the most incredible story every told.

Success in sales presents some great fun and great opportunities. Along the way, you will go some great places and meet some great people.

♦ A Review

President Ronald Reagan & Mike Manley

Secretary of State Hilary Clinton

Senator Jeff Sessions MO.

Speaker Newt Gingridge

Governor Haley Barbour MS.

Senator Bob Barr GA.

Governor Ed Rendell PA.

Governor Jebb Bush FL.

Senator Bob Dole KS.

Senator Nighthorse Campbell AZ   *Republican National Committee*

Jim Nicholson   *General Alexander Haig*   *General Norman*
RNC Chairman   *Schwarzkoph*

Jimmy Hoffa Jr.   *Miss America*   *Helen Thomas, White*
                                                  House correspondent

Candy Crowley CNN   *James Carville & Mary Magdalene*

You need to work hard to master your craft for sure, but when you finally get there, you should enjoy it. You should try to find a good joke for the day and tell it whenever you can most of the time. Whoever you tell it to has a good joke of his or her own, and there you go. Most sales organizations give awards, cash, prizes, trips, and so forth to their producers in appreciation for a job well done. I have traveled the country and most of the world this way. There is sometimes no other choice but to have fun.

AFTERWORD

At this point in this book, given that you actually read it all and do it, you should be very enthused about your company, product, knowledge, confidence, practice, presentation, attributes, perpetual closing abilities, numbers game, discipline, firm commitment to always do the right thing, and ability to avoid obstacles to the point of sale. You know who to follow, and you know how to have fun. All these opportunities await you. My, my, my, what to do now? Throughout this book, I have tried to stay true to the things you must do in a direct sale or any sale for that matter, and I think I did. Always remember, "The Keys to Direct Sales Success."

MORE FRIENDS

ABOUT THE AUTHOR

Mike Manley has more than twenty-seven years experience with direct sales. Starting as an associate with Aflac, he has held district, regional, state, and multiple state sales management positions around the country. He has received every major sales award that Aflac gives its sales agents, including the Fireball, Super Fireball, Triple Crown, and the Gold, Silver, and Bronze Key Club Awards. In 1987, Manley was named the top associate in the United States. He is the recipient of the coveted and prestigious Amos Award. Manley retains district, regional, and state recruiting records. He is a lifetime member in Aflac President's Club for excellence in sales performance. Manley has also worked with Colonial Life and Accident Insurance Company, and he was the regional director for Pennsylvania, New Jersey, and Delaware. Manley continues to sell as an independent insurance broker and remains at the top of the leaderboard today.

Manley is a decorated, six-year United States Army Infantry veteran, and he received the Meritorious Service Medal. In 1984, Manley was named as an Outstanding Young Man in America and recently received the Senatorial Medal of Freedom, the highest honor the Republican members of Congress can bestow on an individual.

Mike Manley currently resides in Jupiter, Florida, with his family.

NOTES

NOTES

NOTES

NOTES

Notes

NOTES

NOTES

NOTES

NOTES

NOTES

NOTES